D0907176

Mitchell Lane
PUBLISHERS

P.O. Box 196
Hockessin, Delaware 19707
Visit us on the web: www.mitchelllane.com
Comments? email us: contactus@mitchelllane.com

ANCIENT SPARTA

PETE DIPRIMIO

EXPLORE
ANCIENT
WORLDS

EXPLORE ANCIENT WORLDS

Ancient Assyria • Ancient Athens
The Aztecs • Ancient Babylon
The Byzantine Empire • The Celts of the British Isles
Ancient China • Ancient Egypt
Ancient India/Maurya Empire • Ancient Sparta

ABOUT THE AUTHOR: Pete DiPrimio is an
award-wining Indiana sports writer, a long-
time freelance writer and a veteran children's
author. He's also a journalism adjunct lecturer
and fitness instructor.

PUBLISHER'S NOTE: The facts on which the story
in this book is based have been thoroughly
researched. Documentation of such research
can be found on page 44. While every possible
effort has been made to ensure accuracy, the
publisher will not assume liability for damages
caused by inaccuracies in the data, and
makes no warranty on the accuracy of the
information contained herein.

Printing   1 2 3 4 5 6 7 8 9

**Library of Congress
Cataloging-in-Publication Data**
DiPrimio, Pete.
  Ancient Sparta / by Pete DiPrimio.
    p. cm.—(Explore ancient worlds)
  Includes bibliographical references and index.
  ISBN 978-1-61228-276-3 (library bound)
  1. Sparta (Extinct city)—History—Juvenile
  literature. 2. Sparta (Extinct city)—Civilization—
  Juvenile literature. I. Title.
  DF261.S8D58 2013
  938'.9—dc23

                                2012009410

eBook ISBN: 9781612282817

PLB

CONTENTS

Spartan warriors took advantage of narrow mountain passes to hold off the larger Persian army.

4

CHAPTER 1

A Fierce Spirit

Wind whipped hard through Leonidas' long dark hair, bringing with it the smell of campfire smoke, seawater, and blood. He shivered despite the summer heat, twisting his shoulders so his men wouldn't notice. He gripped an iron sword in one hand, a bronze helmet in the other. The rocks near the Pass of Thermopylae dug like nails through his leather boots and into the bottoms of his feet. Dawn was breaking and clouds boiled dark and ominous over a treeless mountain. Far below on a grayish-white beach loomed the massive Persian army of Xerxes, who had come to conquer Greece as previous Persian rulers had conquered so much of Asia and North Africa.[1]

"What is your command, my king?" said Dieneces, a wounded soldier standing nearby.

Probably about 50 years old on that August day in 480 BCE, Leonidas had been a king of Sparta for ten years. Now he faced the decision he had been born to make—fight and die as a hero or surrender and live as a coward.[2]

It was no choice at all.

His wife and queen, Gorgo, had given him the order all Spartan women did when their men left for battle: "Return either with your shield, or on it."

In other words, win or die trying.

Unlike most Spartan kings, Leonidas had been trained as a Spartan warrior. He had been starved and beaten, forced to live by lies as well as by truth. He knew discipline and death. He was as battle-tested as any man under his command, but this was a test unlike any other.[3]

The Persian army had anywhere from 50,000 to 250,000 soldiers, plus a giant fleet of ships. Leonidas had 300 Spartans and enough other Greeks to total around 7,000 men. Leonidas had wanted more troops, but the Olympic Games were going on at the time and religious duties required Greek

---

MEDITERRANEAN SEA

ALBANIA

MACEDONIA

BULGARIA

TURKEY

GREECE

Mount Olympus

• Thessaloniki Thassos

Corfu

IONIAN ISLANDS

Cephalonia

IONIAN SEA

Zante

Patras Corinth•

Gulf of Corinth

• Olympia

Peloponnese Peninsula

SPARTA•

100 km
100 miles

Skiathos

SPORADES

Skopelos

Lemnos

Lesvos

AEGEAN SEA

Chios

SARONIC ISLANDS

ATHENS•

Mykonos

Andros

Naxos

CYCLADES

Santorini

DODECANESE

Samos

Kos

SEA OF CRETE

Crete

Rhodes

Karapathos

warriors to participate. Leonidas received only those veterans who could be spared. All had sons who could replace them if they were killed. He was told to hold on until a larger Greek army arrived.[4]

After a lot of arguing, the Greeks decided to make their stand at Thermopylae, a narrow strip of land northwest of Athens where the mountains dropped to within fifty feet of the Aegean Sea. The route would force the Persians into a narrow pass where the Spartans would have a better chance to fight them off.[5]

Before he left, Leonidas consulted the Oracle at Delphi about what he should do. The Oracle was a priestess (called the Pythia) who, according to legend, could see the future through the help of the Greek god Apollo. The priestess would go into a trance and make a prophecy. Priests would write the prophecy into a short poem that was often mysterious.[6]

The Oracle told Leonidas, "People of Sparta, either your city is destroyed by the Persians or it is not and Lakedaimon will mourn a dead king of the Heraklid line. For the might of bulls and lions will not stay the enemy in battle. He has Zeus' might. And I say that he will not stop until he has destroyed one of these two."[7]

In other words, either Sparta would be destroyed or Leonidas would die saving it. Leonidas understood what he had to do.

For six days the Spartans stood their ground, the first four waiting for Xerxes to attack, the next two holding off his army. Three times Xerxes launched an attack. Three times the Greeks stopped them, killing about 20,000 Persians while losing around 2,500 of themselves.[8]

Then a Greek betrayed them, showing the Persians a secret mountain pass that enabled them to get behind Leonidas and his men. That would put Persian troops in front and in back. Those troops would include Xerxes' 10,000-man elite force, called the Immortals. The Greeks called them the Immortals because they believed—though they weren't correct—that each man had a replacement ready. When one died, supposedly the next one took his place so the 10,000 number never changed.[9]

The Spartans knew they were doomed. They were the best in the world, and as fierce as they were, they were surrounded. Leonidas told most of his

7

army to go, leaving only the Spartans, Thebans, and Thespians. They would delay the Persians as long as they could.

In the distance drums began pounding. The Persians were marching up from their seaside camp. A scout told Leonidas that more Persians were coming from the rear. They were trapped. The Spartans began oiling themselves and combing their long hair in a Spartan tradition that helped to prepare them for death. Leonidas jumped onto a rock so everyone could see him. By Spartan law men ate dinner together every night, but he knew they would not live that long. His spies told him that Xerxes had ordered the Immortals to kill him, cut off his head, and crucify his body as a lesson to those who would resist the Persian leader.[10]

"Eat a hearty breakfast, Spartans," he shouted, "for tonight we shall dine in Hades!" It meant they would have dinner in the Underworld.[11]

Immortals were Xerxes' elite warriors.

A Fierce Spirit

Xerxes, the Persian ruler who invaded ancient Greece.

The Spartans roared their approval, then stopped and pointed. An unarmed man wearing the white color of a messenger scrambled down the mountain toward them. Dieneces intercepted him with a raised sword, but Leonidas motioned to let the man approach.

"The great and merciful Xerxes offers you a chance to surrender," the messenger said with bowed head. "Join him and all will be spared. He will make you ruler over all of Greece." To reinforce the point, the messenger also gave him a letter from Xerxes that said, "Hand over your arms."

Leonidas is honored with this statue, called the "Leonidas Monument," near Thermopylae. The inscription says, "Come and take them!" It was his response to Xerxes' command that the Greeks hand over their weapons.

Leonidas grabbed the letter and wrote "Come and take them" on the back.

"Take this to Xerxes," Leonidas said.

The messenger looked stunned. "Do you not understand what you face? We have so many archers their arrows will blot out the sun."

Dieneces jabbed the messenger with his sword, drawing blood.

"Then we shall fight them in the shade," Dieneces said. [12]

Leonidas raised his sword and 300 Spartan warriors raised theirs, shouting loud enough for Xerxes to hear: "Spartans never surrender!"

Battle of Plataea, 479 BCE

Pausanias

The struggle with the Persians came to a head about a year after the Battle of Thermopylae. Persian general Mardonius had about 100,000 troops near the town of Plataea, about 30 miles northwest of Athens. His job was to keep this part of Greece under Persian control. The Greeks weren't about to let that happen. So an army of an estimated 40,000 hoplites (heavily armed Greek soldiers) and a number of more lightly armored men from Sparta, Athens, and several other city-states was sent to drive out the Persians. The Greeks were led by a Spartan general named Pausanias.

Not much happened for more than a week as both sides sized each other up. Then the Persians destroyed the Greeks' supply train and poisoned their wells. Lacking food and water, Pausanias ordered a night-time retreat. The other city-states retreated, but the Spartans and Athenians stayed. Sensing the chance to break the divided Greeks, Mardonius attacked in what became the largest land battle of the Persian War.

Some of his troops went after the Athenians, while others attacked the Spartans. The Spartans used their shields to protect them from Persian archers, then attacked with their phalanx. With the Persians' bows and arrows not doing much damage, they got into hand-to-hand fighting, and had no chance against the Spartans' phalanx. The Persians were driven back.

With the Athenians also winning their fight, the Persians retreated. The Greeks caught and killed Mardonius and thousands of his troops. This Greek victory basically ended the Persian invasion.

Lycurgus inspired the Spartans to form a new kind of warrior society.

CHAPTER 2

Lycurgus Rules

Lycurgus lied with an honest face. He had changed a people, shaken a world, and created a new way of life. Because of him, Sparta would be feared and respected as no other Greek city-state. He would be remembered for all time. Some would see him as a man, others as a myth. Some would love him. Others would hate him.

It didn't matter. In a few moments, it would be over. There was no going back. The Oracle of Delphi had told him so. It all came down to the power of his words.

He gathered the Spartan leaders in a field outside the city. It was about 300 years before Leonidas would fight the Persians. Lycurgus wore a simple white tunic and cracked brown leather sandals. White hair hung past his shoulders. His wrinkled map of a face told of too many long days exposed to the direct sun. A black patch covered the gouged-out eye he suffered years earlier during a street fight in Crete (in his prime he had been a martial arts champion).[1] At his feet was a small white sack that carried all of his belongings. It weighed, perhaps, as much as two loaves of bread.

"What is it that is so important that you have asked all of us here?" a short, fat senator asked. He was Menelon, an unhappy man who had fought Lycurgus' reforms at every turn. Lycurgus thanked the gods this would be the last day he'd ever see him.

Lycurgus' name meant "Wolf-Worker." He was closely linked with Apollo, the god who also had wolfish characteristics and who had a famous temple dedicated to him at Delphi. The Oracle of Delphi was famous throughout the ancient world for her ability to predict the future, and Lycurgus had consulted her well.

Considered the father of Sparta, Lycurgus was like a combination of George Washington and a ruthless dictator.[2] He built stability where there had been uncertainty, but he was old and dying. He would decide how his life ended just as he would make sure everything he had done would not be undone. He would go deep into the mountains surrounding Sparta, to a cave he had discovered as a boy, and stop eating so as to rid himself of everything unclean until the gods took him to Elysium, the Greek heaven.

"We have seen many changes," he said, "and I know it has been hard. I thank you for your support and understanding. Because of you, Sparta will be great."

"No, it is because of you, Lycurgus!" another senator shouted and the crowd roared its approval.

Lycurgus was a natural leader, strong and smart and disciplined. People respected him and he needed all of that respect now.

"There is one last thing I must do," he said. "It is the most important thing of all to ensure Sparta stays great for as long as the sun rises and sets."

"What is it?" a voice shouted out, and more voices joined his. Lycurgus raised his hand again to silence them.

He wanted Sparta to be strong and powerful, but didn't want it to create an empire by conquering and ruling other cities and lands. He believed that a happy nation, like a happy man, comes from virtue, not power or wealth. He wanted Spartans to be self-reliant, free-minded, and disciplined; to live simply and without luxury. So he had pushed through laws that made Sparta unlike any other place on earth. If the laws stayed, Sparta would be great. If not...he didn't want to think about it.

"I will go to Delphi and consult with the Oracle," he said. "I must get wisdom from Apollo himself. Until then I cannot say what it is. But it is

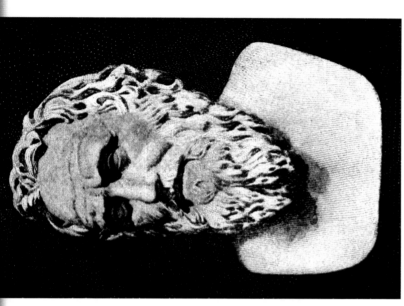

Lycurgus

vital that you here now swear to obey and keep the laws and not change anything until I return."

"Why should we do that?" Menelon asked.

Lycurgus smiled. "Because I asked you to. Is that not enough?"

The crowd cheered Lycurgus and booed the senator. "We swear to Apollo we will obey the laws and not change them until you have returned to us," they shouted. And then, "Long live Lycurgus!"

Lycurgus knew the Spartans would never break their oath. He bowed his head and picked up the small white sack. He did not want the crowd to see his sadness. He would miss many of them.

"When will you return?" a senator asked.

"As soon as I can," he said. It was the last lie he would ever tell.

According to legend, Lycurgus was descended from Hercules, was the second prince in one of two royal families of Sparta, and lived sometime between 800 and 700 BCE.[3] But as a young man he gave up his authority and traveled all over the Mediterranean region. He visited the island of Crete and studied its government, picking out ideas that might help Sparta. He went to Ionia (in modern-day Turkey) and discovered the writings of Homer, taking notes about Homer's thoughts on government and the difference between right and wrong. He went to Egypt and got the idea of separating the military from those who raised crops and did chores.

Lycurgus
Demonstrates
the Benefits
of Education,
1661 painting
by Caesar Van
Everdingen

Meanwhile, Sparta struggled because it kept going back and forth from a democracy to a dictatorship. It needed stability and strength. Leaders contacted Lycurgus, who was determined to change Sparta with a series of reforms called the "Great Rhetra."[4] He wanted to create a society unlike any other.

First, he asked the Oracle at Delphi for guidance. Was this the right thing to do? Yes, the Oracle said. Sparta would become famous throughout the world. The Oracle, according to legend, even gave him specific laws. So Lycurgus returned to the city. He talked to a few of the leading men in Sparta, then a few more, until about thirty joined him. They convinced one of Sparta's two kings, Charilaus, who was actually Lycurgus' nephew, to go along with the reforms.[5]

None of the reforms could be written down. They would have to be remembered, which meant every citizen had to have a good education. Wise judges would explain and resolve any confusion or dispute.[6]

Lycurgus changed the government, the education, the money, and the lifestyle. Spartans lived simply, bravely and fiercely. Because of their oath, they never changed.

Strange Laws

Lycurgus made some laws that seem strange until his reasoning becomes apparent.

One of the weirdest laws involved constructing houses and buildings. Walls were made of sun-baked brick, which was normal. Ceilings, gates, and doors were made of wood, and axes could be the only tools to make them. This limitation produced rough-looking ceilings and doors. Why do that? Because fancy furniture would look out of place if everybody kept it plain. Lycurgus wanted to do away with all luxury.[7]

He also tried to get rid of greed by banning gold and silver. Money was made only of iron bars and coins. The coins were dipped in vinegar to make them brittle.[8] Nobody outside of Sparta wanted them, so nobody sold the Spartans anything. Things like jewelry, art, and other fancy things disappeared.[9] Robbery and bribery stopped because no one wanted the Spartans' money. It also helped keep Sparta isolated, which is what Lycurgus wanted. He didn't want any ideas from other societies interfering with his perfect community.

Spartans were not allowed to travel to other countries and people from other countries were not allowed to visit Sparta. Lycurgus was worried that new ideas and luxuries would make Spartans want to change or get rid of his reforms.[10]

Lycurgus changed the way the Spartans owned land. Previously most of the land and money was owned by the rich few, which left most people poor and angry. Lycurgus divided all the land equally. The rich didn't like it at first, but they adjusted.

A wood axe

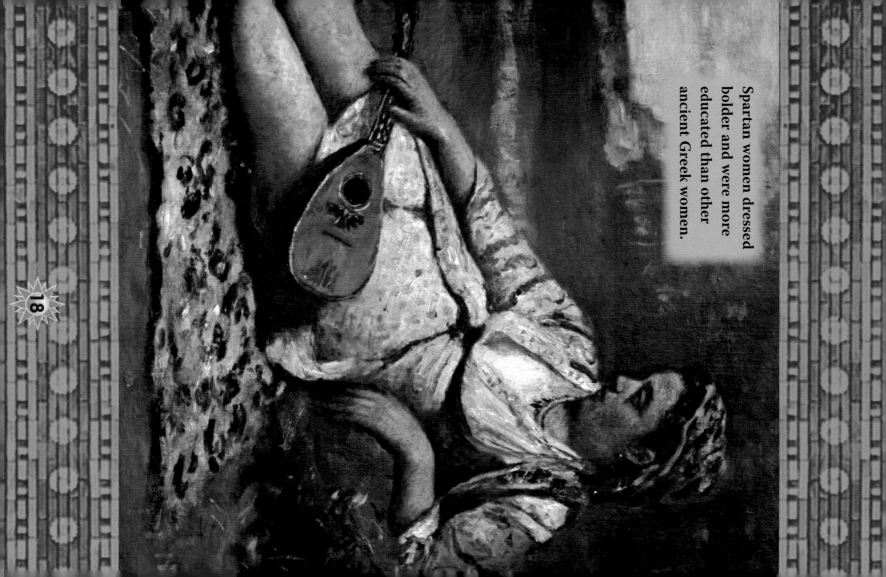

Spartan women dressed bolder and were more educated than other ancient Greek women.

18

3

Cynisca: The Woman Who Conquered Men

Cynisca thrust the horse brush as if it were a sword at the large man with gray hair rimming his egg-shaped head.

"Are you telling me what to do?" she asked in an angry tone. She was fit and tall like most Spartan women, perhaps because they, unlike other Greek women, ate well and exercised often. She had striking blue eyes and a beautiful face to rival another Spartan woman, Helen of Troy, who was so beautiful that she had caused the Trojan War. Streaks of gray framed the edges of Cynisca's dark hair. She acted nothing like her name, which meant "female puppy."[1]

"Everybody has to follow the rules. No exceptions," the man said. He was Gitiadas, chariot race official for the Olympic Games. He nervously kicked at the brown dirt surrounding the horse stalls and dust coated his brown wool chiton. Spartan women made him nervous, this one in particular with her short white tunic that showed more leg and arms than was appropriate. The other Greeks called them "thigh flashers" because of the way they dressed. They didn't know their place like other Greek women. Wind rustled through nearby olive trees. The sun blazed from a cloudless sky in this summer morning of 396 BCE. On the other side of a ridge was the town of Olympia, the site of the Olympics. It was nestled in the mountains in the northwest corner of this Greek peninsula known as

the Peloponnesus. A small brown horse whinnied from the other side of the white fence as if to get Cynisca to resume brushing him.

"I'm not a slave you can order around," Cynisca said. "Agesilaus, tell him."

Another man, who looked very much like Cynisca except in a longer, more conservative white tunic, stroked his dark curly beard. He was the king of Sparta, but he knew who was really in charge. "You don't want to anger my sister," Agesilaus said with a dry tone.

"She has to follow the rules," Gitiadas said. "No women can compete in the Olympics."

Cynisca shook her head and her long hair snapped behind her back like a whip. "Show me where it says I can't enter my chariot team."

Cynisca: The Woman who Conquered Men

Olympia

"You know I can't do that. The rules aren't written down. Nothing is. It's not the Spartan way."

"We're not in Sparta, you fool," she said. "But I'll tell you what the Spartan way is. It's winning. Non-Spartan men don't want me to enter because they're afraid. You're afraid."

Gitiadas balled his hands into fists. "If you were a man, I'd fight you for saying that."

Cynisca moved close enough to hug, and close enough to slug. Her well-defined arms and legs glistened from the oil she'd rubbed on them to keep them clean and healthy. "If you were a man, I'd let you try."

Spartans excelled at chariot racing, and all Olympic sports.

Agesilaus moved between them. As the king, his every act and word carried special importance.[2]

"You speak of Olympic rules," Agesilaus said. "I know them. They say women can't be at the main stadium, where the running and combat events are held. They say women can't directly participate in any events. My sister would do none of those. She has a rider for the chariot. He will race. No rules would be broken."

Gitiadas hesitated. He knew the king was right. It was a loophole in the rules no one had ever tried to use before. Besides, it was not wise to argue with a Spartan king.

"Do as you wish," he said at last. "And forget what I said about fighting you. I was wrong."

"Of course you were wrong," Cynisca said. "You're not a Spartan."

Cynisca reached across the fence to resume brushing the horse, ignoring the buzzing flies and dry August heat. The four-horse chariot race was the next day and she knew she would win. She had bred her horses to win, and they were the swiftest and toughest in all of Greece. She had the best rider, a former slave named Chionis after the great Spartan Olympic champion from more than two hundred years earlier. No one had heard of her rider, but the next day would change that.

Chariot owners never raced in the Olympics.[3] It was too dangerous because of the crashes that often left riders dead or crippled. Some owners hired professional riders, others forced slaves to do it. Cynisca wanted to do her own riding, but there were some rules even she had to follow. Besides, chariot owners were considered the competitors, not the riders. The owners got the prizes and the glory. No woman had ever won in all the years the Olympic Games had been held. Women weren't even allowed to watch the Games.

Cynisca had grown up for this moment. Her father had been a Spartan king and saw to it that she was trained as a Spartan boy would be trained. She had learned to fight and wrestle and do gymnastics.[4] She was 44 years old in this summer of 396 BCE, but if time had slowed her down, no one could tell.

"What are you thinking?" Agesilaus asked. He was four years older, and knew her better than anyone.

"Tomorrow we'll make history," she said with a fierce smile.

Cynisca did make history the next day when her chariot team won. Four

Spartan women usually helped prepare men to enter arenas, but weren't allowed to enter themselves.

Cynisca and her chariot

years later, in 392 BCE, she did it again. She was so proud and had so much influence because of Agesilaus' support that she built a bronze statue of herself, her chariot, and her team in the Temple of Zeus at Olympia. It included an inscription that told of her achievement:

"My father and brothers were Spartan kings,
I won with a team of fast-footed horses, and put up this monument:
I am Cynisca: I am the only woman in all Greece to have won this wreath."[5]

Cynisca also got a hero's shrine in a sacred grove of trees in Sparta, an honor normally given only to kings. She was the only woman to ever receive that honor.

Her achievement inspired another Spartan woman, Euryleonis, to win the two-horse chariot race in the 366 BCE Olympic Games.[6] While most Greeks didn't like to compete with women, Spartan men did because it showed that their women were tougher than other Greek men.

Cynisca was wrong about one thing—not many remember the name of her chariot racer. But they remember her.

Gorgo and Spartan Women

Gorgo ruled her house and the man who ruled Sparta. This wasn't surprising. Spartan women were known as much for the strength of their spirit as of their bodies. At home they had the last word, and the men, the fiercest warriors of the ancient world, knew their place.

Gorgo was queen of Sparta and wife of Leonidas, the Spartan king and the leader of the 300 men who died at Thermopylae. She is, in some ways, as famous as her husband. The great Greek historian, Plutarch, wrote this about her:

"Why are you Spartan women the only ones who can rule men?" she was once asked.

"Because we are also the only ones who give birth to men," she said.[7]

Gorgo, who was probably born between 510 and 506 BCE, also was the daughter of one king (Cleomenes I) and the mother of another king (Pleistarchus). She represented the ideal Spartan woman.

Why were Spartan women more dominant in society than other Greek women? Here are some reasons:

1. Spartan girls were well-educated in arts and athletics.
2. Spartan women were encouraged to develop their minds.
3. Spartan women owned more than a third of the land.
4. Spartan women married at a later age and were closer in age to their husbands.
5. Spartan women did all the childrearing until age 7, when society took charge of the boys. Fathers did little with their children.

Gorgo of Sparta

An agricultural valley in Sparta

CHAPTER 4

Spartan Life

What was it like to live in Sparta?

The people were divided into three classes. The Spartiates were the warriors and landowners, the ones who held political power and full citizenship. There were never more than 10,000 of them. All they did was train for the military, hunt, swim, breed animals, take care of their land, and wage war. They weren't allowed to have any other jobs.[1]

The perioikoi (which means "those who live around the area") were tax-paying traders, farmers, and artists who lived in dozens of towns near Sparta itself. They only had to join the Spartan army when asked.

The helots were like serfs or peasants (they did all the farming, cleaning, and things nobody else wanted to do) and didn't have any rights. There were a lot more of them than there were Spartiates and perioikoi. They lived in the land around Sparta and were terrorized into obeying Spartan laws.[2]

Ancient Sparta produced a lot of art, poetry, music, and dancing, but Lycurgus did away with most of that except for dancing.[3]

Early on Sparta was known mostly for farming. It produced wine and olive oil, barley, wheat, figs, and goat cheese. Sheep and goats provided wool and meat. That changed once Lycurgus took charge.

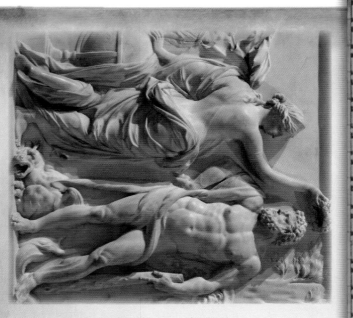

Lycurgus, like all Spartan kings, was said to be a descendant of Hercules, the Greek mythological strongman portrayed here receiving his crown.

Sparta, like the United States, believed in a government that had a balance of power. It had two kings from the Agiad and Eurypontid families who were, legend said, descendants of Hercules. Both kings had the same power.[4]

Lycurgus added a 28-member senate (only for men 60 years old and older) that had the same power as the kings and served for life. There also was a council of 300 representatives. Later, five leaders (called ephors) were elected each year. They took some of the kings' powers.[5]

Only citizens (men over the age of 30) could vote, but only the senate could decide when a vote could be taken. Votes were taken in an open field outside the city. Nearby in a small house without windows judges rated the applause each candidate received to determine the winner. To make sure there was no cheating, the judges didn't know the vote order so they didn't know who was getting the applause.[6]

Lycurgus' ideas on education were called "agoge" (which means "raising," like one might raise cattle).[7] For boys, the goal was to turn them into the toughest and nastiest warriors of the ancient world.

Men lived with each other in barracks until they were 30, even if they were married, and had to eat together at night. During those dinners, the eating area was divided into tables of fifteen men. Each man had to bring a certain amount of food and wine every month. Boys were allowed to be at these tables so they could learn how to talk like men. That included saying what was on their minds. To make sure men weren't afraid to speak up, the oldest man would tell them at the start of the meal that, "Through this (door), no words go out." In other words, what was said at the table stayed at the table.[8]

Whenever somebody new wanted to join a table, the others voted on it. Each man threw a ball of dough into a bowl. If he wanted the newcomer to join, he left the ball alone. If he didn't, he squashed it flat. If any ball was squashed, the newcomer couldn't join.[9]

Spartan girls were raised to become strong, healthy, smart women so they could have strong, healthy, smart babies. They ran and exercised, wrestled and rode horses, usually at the same time and place as the boys. They sometimes danced naked in front of all the young men. That made the girls ashamed to be weak or fat and proud to show their beauty. They sang songs that praised strong, brave men, and made fun of weak, cowardly ones. As a result, boys would do everything they could to impress girls.

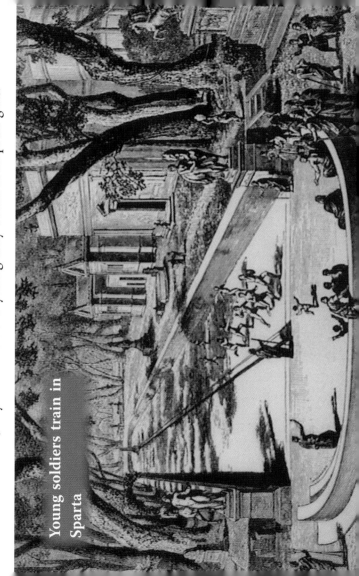

Young soldiers train in Sparta

Spartan women rarely married before age 20 and a man couldn't live with a woman until he was 30, although he could marry earlier. If he got married before 30, or just wanted to meet his woman as lovers, it had to be in secret, probably during the day because the man had to be in his barracks at night. If they were caught, they would be made fun of.[10]

Spartans married, not for love as much as to produce healthy babies. Weddings were done in secret and only involved the bride and her family in a private ceremony. Then her hair was cut off and she dressed in male clothes. The groom secretly met with her, then went back to his barracks.[11]

A Spartan woman has her child examined.

In Sparta, children belonged to society and not to parents. Lycurgus wanted the best men and women to get together so they'd produce the best children. Lycurgus figured men bred their dogs and horses to get the best offspring, so why not do it with people?

When a child was born, it was taken to a council of elders for examination. If it was sick or weak or handicapped, it was left in the wilderness to die. The Spartans had no use for the weak. Healthy children were washed in wine because Spartans believed it would make them strong.[12]

Spartan boys were taken from their homes at age 7 to begin training to become soldiers. They learned to read and write, but mostly they learned how to obey, fight, and endure pain. They were often tested to see who the best fighters were.[13]

While most other ancient Greek women had to stay in the home, Spartan women went out to shop, conduct business, help with their husband's estate, and exercise. They were very independent.

Spartan Wit

Philip of Macedonia

Spartans were almost as famous for what they said as for how well they fought. That's impressive because nobody wanted to mess with the Spartans in battle or in sports. A sharp mind was considered just as important as a fit body. Spartans learned to pack a lot of punch into each sentence, and to keep those sentences short. Children were taught to stay silent, so when they finally spoke, what they said was important.

One of the most famous examples of Spartan wit came in 339 BCE. Philip of Macedonia, the father of Alexander the Great and also a great conqueror in his own right, was set to invade Laconia, the region that included Sparta. Seeking to intimidate his enemies, Philip wrote to the Spartans, "If I enter Laconia, I shall level it to the ground."

The Spartans replied, "If."[14]

That short response is known as "laconic," which describes statements that are short, sharp, and smart.

An Athenian once joked that sword-swallowers used Spartan swords because they were so short. A Spartan shot back: "We find them long enough to reach the heart of our enemies."[15]

A man once told Lycurgus that Sparta should be a democracy. Lycurgus replied: "Begin with your own family."[16]

Sparta was one of the few Greek city-states constructed without a protective wall. Some people wondered if that was a mistake, if a wall should be built to stop invaders. Lycurgus said, "A wall of men, instead of bricks, is best."[17]

Mystras, an ancient fort-like town built into the steep foothills of Mt. Taygetos, became important after Sparta was destroyed in 396 CE.

CHAPTER 5

The Warrior Way

Alexandros braced for the whip. He shivered from the cold that slashed through his thin tunic like a knife.

"Show me your back," the iren said in a harsh voice. He was a tall, densely muscled man who clutched a black whip so tightly his knuckles had turned white. Alexandros didn't know his name. None of the Spartan boys did. The iren led their group through fear and intimidation. He would turn them into soldiers or they would die. There was no other option.

Alexandros was a month past his twelfth birthday, which meant he was a month into the Spartan military education. The boys joined groups run by "irens." These were twenty-year-old men much like today's drill sergeants.[1] They trained the boys for six years and it was tough. The boys could only wear one cloak—no shoes or underwear or jackets, even in winter. They slept with their groups, making beds of reeds they gathered from rivers. Sometimes they were beaten for no apparent reason. They were expected to take it without crying out because that would show weakness.[2]

Alexandros' stomach rumbled. His hunger was so great it even overcame his fear. It was why he had tried to steal food from another group. The iren never gave them enough food. Spartans believed starving boys at times helped them grow taller because too much food made them fat. The iren encouraged them to steal from others. Alexandros had tried, but his plan was poor and his execution was worse. He had waited until all the boys were asleep, and all the irens were busy talking. He slipped out looking for leftovers. A barking dog alerted the irens and now he faced the consequences.

"You have to be smart," the iren said. "You have to plan. That's why the gods gave you a brain."

"Yes, sir," Alexandros said. His crime was not in trying to steal, but in getting caught.

"I will be kind. You will get twelve lashes. You will not cry out. Do you understand?"

Crying out was not the Spartan way. A famous legend told of a young Spartan boy who stole a fox, planning to kill and eat it. He ran into some Spartan soldiers and hid the fox under his tunic. While the soldiers grilled him on why he wasn't in school, the fox began chewing into the boy's stomach. If the boy cried out, the soldiers would know he had stolen the fox and would beat him. So he kept silent and let the fox do its worst.

The moral—it was okay to lie, cheat, and steal. It was NOT okay to get caught.[3]

Alexandros had been caught. He would take his punishment and learn. He would prove he could be a fierce warrior like his father and grandfather. That meant he would eventually join the Crypteia, a type of spy network, and be sent into the countryside to find and kill any helots who looked like they might become leaders and a danger to Sparta.

It was ruthless, but it was the Spartan way.

The whip slashed open his back. Again, and again, and again. He did not cry out.

Spartans liked war because it gave them a break from their brutal training. They were allowed to take time to comb their hair,

A Spartan shield displayed in an Athens museum

which was kept long. Lycurgus said that long hair added beauty to a good face and terror to an ugly one.[4]

Spartan soldiers, called hoplites, had advantages beyond their rigorous training. They loved to spy and get information, and did both very well. Their helmets, swords, shields, and long spears were the best in the ancient world. They fought in a phalanx, which was a large formation that involved a coordinated mass movement. They would line up next to each other in groups up to 12 rows deep. They all had raised wooden shields that formed an unbroken wall, and advanced toward their enemies with their spears extended. When a man up front was injured or killed, the soldier behind him moved up to take his place.[5]

Many ancient armies just gathered mobs of men who wanted to fight one on one. The Spartans fought as a unit so that even a small number of hoplites could beat much larger armies. They used their phalanxes to crush the enemy or terrorize them into retreat or surrender.[6]

Before battles the king would make a sacrifice to the Muses (goddesses of the arts) to remind the warriors their actions would be judged so they should act bravely. Spartans also used inspirational music to prepare themselves. They marched toward the enemy singing to the sounds of flutes. Terpander, a poet of that era, said, "(The Spartans') spear was strong, their music sweet, and Justice kept an honored seat."[7]

The Spartans attacked until victory was certain. They never slaughtered a retreating enemy, only those who kept fighting. Enemies would often flee when the Spartans appeared, which made war a lot easier.[8]

Today, Sparta is a sleepy town with clean air and fresh food. Its buildings are built low to preserve the views of the surrounding mountains. It has a population of around 18,000 and is known for its olives and oranges. The warrior spirit is gone, but not forgotten.

Just like Ancient Sparta.

Old City Hall in modern Sparta

A Little History

Sparta began as a collection of settlements that gradually merged into an unimpressive city on the banks of the Eurotas River. Unlike most other Greek cities, the Spartans didn't build a wall. They thought their fierce fighters could handle any invaders. In addition, the city was surrounded by one of the highest mountain ranges in Greece.

Long-simmering disagreements with the other dominant Greek power, Athens, led to the Peloponnesian War in 431 BCE. The conflict ended in 404 BCE when Athens surrendered. Sparta was master of all Greece. This mastery didn't last long. In 394 BCE, the Spartan fleet was beaten by the combined navies of Thebes, Athens, Corinth, and Argos. In 371 BCE, a full-strength Spartan army lost for the first time against Thebes.

Sparta never recovered. In 339 BCE, Sparta and all of Greece was finally overwhelmed by the armies of Macedonia, a kingdom just north of Greece that became a power under Philip II and his more famous son, Alexander the Great. They got rid of all of Lycurgus' laws. Those laws were restored by the Romans after they conquered Greece around 146 BCE. Sparta's legendary endurance was turned into freak shows for tourists who watched men tortured (usually being whipped) without crying.[9]

Few Spartan ruins remain today. One is the tomb of Leonidas, who died fighting the Persians. Others include walls of a Spartan theater, the foundation of a bridge, and a four-sided building made of huge blocks of stone.

Spartan hoplite soldier

Spartan Craft: Spartan Shield

The Spartan soldier, or hoplite, carried a large wooden Spartan Shield into battle. This is a very simple craft.

MATERIALS

- Large piece of heavy cardboard
- Two strips of heavy cardboard
- Tape
- Pencil
- Length of string
- Scissors or craft knife
- Crayons or poster paint

DIRECTIONS

1. Draw a large circle on a piece of cardboard, either tracing around a large container or fastening a pencil to a length of string and using it as a simple compass.

2. Cut out the circle with scissors or craft knife.

3. Many ancient Greek shields had a decorative border so you can either color the rim of the circle or cut out another slightly larger circle from different colored cardboard and glue the two together.

4. Decorate your shield. One possibility is a scene from Greek mythology. You can also use a smaller circle of poster board and draw an ancient Spartan design.

5. To hold your shield, cut out two strips of cardboard and attach them to the back. Your forearm will go under one of the strips and you'll grab hold of the other.

39

Spartan Recipe: Greek Muller

This is an ancient Greek recipe taken from the *Taste Greek* magazine.

INGREDIENTS

6 small or 3 large red mullets, cleaned

2 handfuls of fresh herbs, finely chopped (thyme, spearmint, coriander, marjoram, parsley, rosemary). If you do not have fresh herbs, use one soupspoon of each.

3 soupspoons olive oil

Juice of one lemon

Salt and pepper

DIRECTIONS

1. Mix herbs together with oil, lemon juice, and salt and pepper.

2. Spread the mixture on the belly and the outside of the mullets.

3. Line a pan with aluminum foil and put the fish on top.

4. Grill the fish 4–10 minutes on each side, according to the size of the fish.

5. Sprinkle continuously with lemon juice.

6. Grill until the meat easily comes away from the bone.

7. Serve immediately with bread and green salad.

Historical Timeline of Sparta

2000–1600 Middle Bronze Age takes place.

1600–1100 Late Bronze Age (Mycenaean Age) takes place.

1193–1183 Possible dates when the Trojan War, pitting Greeks against the city of Troy, takes place.

1000 Dorians begin settling Sparta and Laconia.

800 Town of Sparta begins expansion.

800 Approximate time that Lycurgus, the father of Sparta, is born.

776 The Olympic Games begin.

730 Approximate time when Lycurgus dies.

669 Sparta is defeated by Argos at the Battle of Hysiae.

550 Cyrus II the Great founds the Persian Empire.

546 Sparta defeats Argos at the Battle of the Champions.

530 Approximate date on which Leonidas is born.

490 Athenians defeat Persians at the Battle of Marathon, Leonidas becomes Spartan king.

480 Spartans are defeated by Persians at Thermopylae.

479 Pausanias, a Spartan, commands victorious Greek forces against the Persians at the Battle of Plataea.

478 Pausanius captures Byzantium from the Persians.

476 Pausanius is driven from Byzantium by Cimon.

464 Earthquake rocks Sparta and leads to a revolt by the helots.

431 Peloponnesian war pitting Sparta against Athens begins.

425 Spartan defenders of the island of Sphacteria surrender to Athenians after a long siege, sending shock waves through the Greek world because Spartans never surrender.

404 Sparta wins Peloponnesian War.

394 Combined navies of Thebes, Corinth, Athens, and Argos defeat Spartan fleet at the Battle of Cnidus.

371 Spartans defeated by Thebans, who are led by Epaminondas.

222 Sparta is occupied for first time ever, by forces led by Antigonus III Doson of Macedon.

146 Romans conquer Greece, which becomes a Roman province.

All dates BCE

CHAPTER ONE – A FIERCE SPIRIT

1. "Peloponnese Guide: Sparta ancient and modern," http://www.greeceathensaegeaninfo.com/p_laconia_city_sparta.htm
2. N.S. Gill, "King Leonidas of Sparta (reigned c. 490 – 480 BCE)," http://ancienthistory.about.com/cs/people/g/leonidas.htm
3. "Sparta in Literature."
4. Robert Wilde, "Historical Myths: The 300 Who Held Thermopylae," http://europeanhistory.about.com/od/ancienteurope/a/histmyths2.htm
5. TimeFrame 600–400 BC, A Soaring Spirit, Time-Life Books editors, (Alexandria, Virginia: Time-Life Books, 1987), pp. 70–71.
6. _____, Reader's Digest Quest for the Past (Pleasantville, New York: Reader's Digest Association, 1984), p. 93.
7. N.S. Gill, "King Leonidas of Sparta."
8. Paul Cartledge, The Spartans: The World of the Warrior Heroes of Ancient Greece (New York: Vintage Books, 2004), p. 258.
9. Ibid., p. 128.
10. Ibid., p. 259.
11. Ibid.
12. Ibid., p. 129.

CHAPTER TWO – LYCURGUS RULES

1. Paul Cartledge, The Spartans: The World of the Warrior Heroes of Ancient Greece (New York: Vintage Books, 2004), p. 258.
2. Ibid., p. 32.
3. Plutarch, "Lycurgus, The Father of Sparta, (circa 800 B.C.)," http://www.e-classics.com/lycurgus.htm
4. Cartledge, The Spartans, p. 64.
5. "Ancient Sparta," http://www.mlahanas.de/Greeks/Cities/AncientSparta.html
6. "Sparta in Literature," http://www.enotes.com/sparta-literature-criticism/sparta-literature
7. Cartledge, The Spartans, p. 60.
8. Ibid., p. 62.
9. Ibid., p. 64.
10. N.S. Gill, "Lycurgus," About.com Guide. http://ancienthistory.about.com/cs/greecehellas1/a/lycurgussparta.htm

CHAPTER THREE – CYNISCA: THE WOMAN WHO CONQUERED MEN

1. Cathy Ann Smith, "Spartan Women – Olympic Winner Cynisca of Sparta," http://www.suite101.com/content/cynisca-of-sparta---first-woman-to-win-an-olympic-gold-medal-a265634
2. N.S. Gill, "Cynisca of Sparta," About.com Guide. http://ancienthistory.about.com/od/sparta/g/Cynisca.htm
3. Smith, "Spartan Women."

4. Paul Cartledge, *The Spartans: The World of the Warrior Heroes of Ancient Greece* (New York: Vintage Books, 2004), p. 37.
5. Ibid., pp. 212–213.
6. Ibid., pp. 215–216.
7. Smith, "Spartan Women."

CHAPTER FOUR — SPARTAN LIFE

1. Plutarch, "Lycurgus, The Father of Sparta, (circa 800 B.C.)." http://www.e-classics.com/lycurgus.htm
2. "Ancient Sparta" http://www.mlahanas.de/Greeks/Cities/AncientSparta.html
3. Plutarch, "Lycurgus."
4. Ibid.
5. Ibid.
6. Ibid.
7. Ibid.
8. Ibid.
9. Ibid.
10. Helena P. Schrader, "Scenes From a Spartan Marriage," *Sparta: Journal of Ancient Spartan and Greek History*, Volume 6 #1, July 10. Markoulakis Publications. http://elysiumgates.com/~helena/marriagescenes.html
11. Ibid.
12. Plutarch, "Lycurgus."
13. Ibid.
14. _____, Reader's Digest Quest for the Past (Pleasantville, New York: Reader's Digest Association, 1984), p. 99.
15. Plutarch, "Lycurgus."
16. Ibid.
17. Ibid.

CHAPTER FIVE — THE WARRIOR WAY

1. "Peloponnese Guide: Sparta ancient and modern." http://www.greeceathensaegeaninfo.com/p_laconia_city_sparta.htm
2. "Ancient Sparta Geography." http://library.thinkquest.org/07aug/01367/geography.htm
3. "Education in Ancient Greece." http://greece.mrdonn.org/education.html
4. Plutarch, "Lycurgus, The Father of Sparta, (circa 800 B.C.)." http://www.e-classics.com/lycurgus.htm
5. _____, *TimeFrame 600–400 BC, A Soaring Spirit* (Alexandria, Virginia: Time-Life Books, 1987), p. 39.
6. Ibid., p. 48.
7. Plutarch, "Lycurgus."
8. Ibid.
9. _____, Reader's Digest Quest for the Past (Pleasantville, New York: Reader's Digest Association, 1984), p. 99.

43

Further Reading

"Ancient Sparta Economy," http://en.wikipedia.org/wiki/Ancient_sparta

"Ancient Sparta in Literature," http://www.enotes.com/sparta-literature-criticism/sparta-literature.

"Ancient Sparta Religion," http://www.megaessays.com/viewpaper/15314.html

Lahanas, Michael, "Ancient Greek Military Technology," http://www.mlahanas.de/Greeks/WarTech.htm

Ford, Michael. *Birth of a Warrior: Spartan Quest*. New York: Working Partners, Walker Publishing Co., 2008.

———. *Legacy of Blood: Spartan Quest*. New York: Working Partners, Walker Publishing Co., 2009

———. *The Fire of Ares: Spartan Quest*. New York: Working Partners, Walker Publishing Co., 2008

McLeese, Don and Chris Marrinan. *Spartans*. (Warriors: Illustrated History). Vero Beach, Fla.: Rourke Publishing Co, 2009.

Morris, Ian McGregor. *Leonidas: Hero of Thermopylae*. New York: Rosen, 2003.

Park, Louise and Timothy Love. *The Spartan Hoplites* (*Ancient & Medieval People*). Tarrytown, N.Y.: Marshall Cavendish Children's Books, 2009.

Powell, Anton. *Ancient Greece* (*Cultural Atlas for Young People*). New York: Chelsea House, 2007.

Sievert, Terry. *The 300: The Battle of Thermopylae*. Mankato, Minnesota: Edge Books, 2009.

"Spartan Women," http://www.fscclub.com/history/fame-sparta-e.shtml

Books

Bauer, Susan Wise. *The History of the Ancient World*. New York: W.W. Norton, 2007.

Bradford, Ernle. *Thermopylae: The Battle for the West*. Cambridge, Massachusetts: DaCapo Press, 2004.

Cantor, Norman F. *Antiquity: From the Birth of Sumerian Civilization to the Fall of the Roman Empire*. New York: Harper Perennial, 2007.

Cartledge, Paul. *The Spartans: The World of the Warrior Heroes of Ancient Greece*. New York: Vintage Books, 2004.

Pomeroy, Sarah B. *Spartan Women*. Oxford, United Kingdom: Oxford University Press, 2002.

Powell, Anton. *Classical Sparta: Techniques Behind Her Success*. New York: Routledge, 1989.

———. *Reader's Digest Quest for the Past*. Pleasantville, New York: Reader's Digest Association, 1984.

———. *TimeFrame 600–400 BC, A Soaring Spirit*. Alexandria, Virginia: Time-Life Books, 1987.

On the Internet

"A History of Ancient Greece, Sparta," http://history-world.org/sparta.htm

"Ancient Greek recipe," http://www.greek-recipe.com/static/ancient/ancientrecipes.html

"Ancient Greek Shield," http://www.activityvillage.co.uk/make_a_greek_shield.htm

"Ancient Sparta," http://www.mlahanas.de/Greeks/Cities/AncientSparta.html

"Ancient Sparta Education," http://greece.mrdonn.org/education.html

"Ancient Sparta Geography," http://www.icsd.k12.ny.us/legacy/highschool/socstud/global2_review/ancient_greece.htm

"Ancient Sparta Geography," http://library.thinkquest.org/07aug/01367/geography.htm

"Ancient Sparta Government," http://www.historylink102.com/greece3/sparta-goverment.htm

Gill, N.S., "Cynisca of Sparta." About.com Guide. http://ancienthistory.about.com/od/sparta/g/Cynisca.htm

Gill, N.S., "Lycurgus," About.com Guide. http://ancienthistory.about.com/cs/greecehellas11/a/lycurgussparta.htm

Gill, N.S., "King Leonidas of Sparta (reigned c. 490 – 480 BCE)," Ancient/Classical History Glossary. http://ancienthistory.about.com/cs/people/g/leonidas.htm

Guisepi, Robert, "A History of Ancient Greece Legacy," http://history-world.org/greece%20legacy.htm

"Peloponnese Guide: Sparta ancient and modern." http://www.greeceathensaegeaninfo.com/p_laconia_city_sparta.htm

Plutarch, "Lycurgus, The Father of Sparta, (75 BCE)," http://www.e-classics.com/lycurgus.htm

Schrader, Helena P., "Scenes From a Spartan Marriage," Sparta: Journal of Ancient Spartan and Greek History, Volume 6 #1, July 10, Markoulakis Publications. http://elysiumgates.com/~helena/marriagescenes.html

"Spartan Art Examples," http://www.sikyon.com/Sparta/Art/sparta_peg03.html

"Sparta, Dorian Ancient Greece and Lacedaemon," http://www.fjkluth.com/sparta.html#Myth

"Sparta Earthquake," http://virtualglobetrotting.com/map/464-bce-sparta-earthquake-epicenter/

Spartan Women – Olympic Winner Cynisca of Sparta, http://www.suite101.com/content/cynisca-of-sparta---first-woman-to-win-an-olympic-gold-medal-a265634

Sparta web links, http://www.historylink102.com/greece3/index.htm

Wilde, Robert, "Historical Myths: The 300 Who Held Thermopylae," About.com Guide. http://europeanhistory.about.com/od/ancienteurope/a/histmyths2.htm

"Women in Sparta," http://www.womenintheancientworld.com/women%20in%20sparta.htm

Glossary

agoge (uh-GO-jee)—Raising; the Spartan method of education.

barracks (BARE-rucks)—Building used to house soldiers.

chiton (KY-tuhn)—A sewn tunic.

crucify (CREW-suh-fie)—Execute by nailing or binding the hands and feet of a person to a cross.

ephors (EE-forz)—Five elected Spartan leaders who took some of the power of the kings.

helots (HEE-luhtz)—Peasants and serfs of Sparta.

hoplites (HAWP-lightz)—Greek soldiers, named for their shields, which were called hoplons.

irens (EE-ruhnz)—Twenty-year-old Spartan men who commanded groups of boys during the boys' military training.

laconic (luh-CAW-nik)—Describing statements that are short and curt, using as few words as possible.

Olympic Games (oh-LIHM-pik GAYMZ)—Famous Greek competition that started in 776 BCE and was held every four years to honor the god Zeus.

perioikoi (pehr-ee-OY-koy)—Free but non-citizen residents of Sparta who lived near the city.

phalanx (FAY-langks)—Rectangular body of troops moving in close formation that demands discipline from each man.

prophecy (PRAW-fuh-see)—Prediction about the future.

Pythia (PIH-thee-uh)—Priestess of the Oracle of Delphi who claimed to be able to foretell the future.

rhetra (REH-truh)—Any kind of saying or pronouncement.

Spartiates (SPAHR-shee-itz)—Spartan citizens who have undergone military training.

thigh flashers (THY FLAA-sherz)—Uncomplimentary term used by other Greeks to describe Spartan women who wore short tunics that showed a lot of skin.

tunic (TOO-nick)—Simple garment that slips on over the head and is knee-length or longer, often belted at the waist.